Positiv

CW01522709

A Step Beyond Positive Thinking

By
Matt Morris, CPCC

Table Of Contents

Introduction

Have you ever entered a room, looked around it and as you make eye contact with others, you begin to feel the energy shift to things like hostility, anger, and guilt? You can feel the negative emotions drain you and you begin to feel your energy sucked right out of you. Now imagine stepping inside that same room, making eye contact and feeling the energy shift to feelings of excitement, happiness, and comfort – feelings of positivity.

What if it could always be like this? What if these feelings were your own perceptions of the situation – meaning that the people were always neutral, but you had a preconceived negative view that people would be thinking negative thoughts of you? Imagine how good it would feel if you were able to flip these negative thoughts to positive ones so that people were always excited and happy to see you because you are filled with positivity. You feel better and much more confident around people, and more importantly you feel much better being with yourself.

If positivity has the power to *completely* shift the feelings, imagine the effects it can have on you as an individual. If you allow yourself to have positivity at the core of who you are as a person, imagine how awesome life would be. Imagine how many people will enjoy being in your presence, how much happier you will feel going to work and even doing mundane tasks. Imagine how great it would feel to get out of a negative slump that's keeping you from moving forward in life.

Positivity brings so much more happiness into people's' lives. It also brings more abundance and the power to attract more into your life including better people, more wealth, and improved inner thoughts. Many of the happiest and most successful people used the power of positive thinking. Some of these people include: Dr. Wayne Dyer, Nelson Mandela, Benjamin Franklin, Mahatma Gandhi, and Isaac Newton.

Positive thinking needs to be a daily practice. It will not happen overnight, but rather it needs to be a conscious effort of being aware of your thoughts and statements to determine if they are coming from a negative or a positive place. Being consciously aware of your thoughts is the first step before it can enter the unconscious mind and become a habit. It is believed that it takes 30 days of effort to form a habit. Therefore, if you take the steps and apply the strategies you'll read about in this book for a consistent 30 days, you will be well on your way to thinking more positively, feeling happier, and attracting more into your life.

Chapter 1: The Road to Positivity

"Keep your thoughts positive because your thoughts become your words. Keep your words positive because your words become your behavior. Keep your behavior positive because your behavior becomes your habits. Keep your habits positive because your habits become your values. Keep your values positive because your values become your destiny."

-Mahatma Gandhi

Everything happens for a reason and many things can change your life. They can knock you down or they can lift you up, but at the end of the day, it all depends on you. It's all in your mind. You, your neighbor, your workmates and your friends all experience the same thing but what makes it different is how you accept, react to, and view the circumstance.

Every human experience has two dimensions, just like a coin with two sides. It has both a negative component and a positive one, and one weighs heavier than the other, each one bearing different results. When you flip a coin and hold it in your hand, you only see one side, but it doesn't mean that you only have one option. There is another side that exists, and it is up to you to flip it around to train yourself to become a positive thinker.

For example, if you did not get accepted during your job interview, there are two things that you can do. You can give up the job hunt and tell yourself that you are a failure. You can stop hoping that you will be successful in your career and you can stay right where you are. Or you can exit the interview room, hold your head high and tell yourself that the job isn't right for you; you will get something better. With this, you went on to look for another job hoping that you succeed in your endeavor. If you choose the first, you automatically lose the chance for success. It is depriving yourself of the opportunity to be happy. The opposite is true for the second option. Choosing the second option means taking steps to bring you closer toward your goal.

When you have been going through something negative for a long period of time, such as a divorce or "hopeless" job hunt, you've surely heard people telling you that there is a light at the end of the tunnel. This cliché statement is true in that the bad will not last forever, and that you need to have hope.

Believing that a positive thing would come out of something negative is not easy. It may sound miraculous event and people have the tendency to be skeptic about it. How can a bad thing yield a good thing? The thing is what you are going through is not really negative. The negativity of it all is just a product of your mind. It will only become negative once you let yourself believe that it is.

Though it is also true that optimism is not just something that can be achieved overnight, it is something that you can achieve with time and practice. You may have been thinking that optimism is just a matter of the mind.

Well, there's some truth to it but not entirely. Optimism is also something that you do and say. It can be developed with the words you choose to use, and the thoughts you choose to let enter your mind.

Focus on your goal

In everything that you do, nothing will make you closer to your goal than focusing on it. Always keep your goal in mind so you don't lose your way. When you fail the job interview, don't think of it as losing your chance to succeed. Keeping the goal in mind will help you stay motivated as you work for it. For example, maybe you need to get job to support yourself, your family, buy a house, get that car you've dreamed about for years, etc. What is your motivation?

Focus gives you direction and when you know where you are going, even if you get lost along the way, you will still get back on track. Remember how people tell you that it's better late than never? It practically means the same thing here. The ability to remind yourself of why you are doing something has power in itself and can reenergize you.

Gratitude

Gratitude goes a long way. I believe gratitude and happiness are closely tied together. When your grateful for things or qualities you possess you're much more likely to create happiness in your life. For example, you might be grateful for the conversation you had yesterday with a friend or relative; or you might be grateful for your ability to communicate effectively with your co-workers, explaining how your ideas are imperative to the success of a particular project. Even being grateful for the things people take for granted, such as food to eat or the ability to walk or being loved, can bring in a refreshing sense of joy and happiness.

Happiness is not always getting what you want when you want it. Often times, it means being content and appreciating what you have. This might get you asking how in the world you can appreciate something like failing a job interview. It does not mean you're a failure, it simply means that you were not the person they were looking for and that there is something better out there for you.

Maybe you can think of the interview as practice and with each interview you have, the more confident and better you will get; maybe you learned something from the interaction or from your experience that you can be appreciative of or grateful for, allowing yourself to improve for your next interview you and learn from your mistakes.

Condition yourself

For a machine to function properly it needs conditioning. Your body, in order to optimally function, needs a warm-up every morning. This principle equally holds true in the way you live your life. That is where a ritual or routine can make a world of difference. What are a few things you can do to condition yourself to being happy every morning?

A few examples might include: 50 jumping jacks to get your blood flowing and feeling energized; or being grateful for being alive and breathing; or positive affirmations to remind yourself of the amazing qualities you have.

Be Persistent and Resilient

Life is a journey. If you don't keep moving, you'll get left behind. Always push yourself to try out new things and challenge yourself to keep moving forward even when the times get tough. There may be obstacles along the way, but you can always knock them down. You are naturally creative and resourceful. You will find your way around them and you have the ability to overcome them.

Don't just react; respond

Reaction is an immediate response to a situation. It is like a reflex that is automatic when you encounter something. When you accidentally touch a hot stove, you reflexively remove your hands from it. Though this reflex is a natural protective mechanism of the body, not everything can be managed with this simple reflex. Sometimes, to be able to protect yourself, you must think first before acting, or respond instead of react.

When you are hungry, you react by grabbing any food that you see. When you respond, you think of ways to get food in the shortest time possible and ways to avoid being hungry in the future. If you want to be an optimistic person, it is not enough that you just react to the situation. Don't just cry or give up or stop moving. Respond to every failure by thinking of ways that you can succeed the next time you encounter the same adversity. That is how we grow as individuals.

Chapter 2: Ways to a Stress-Free Life

"Adopting the right attitude can convert a negative stress into a positive one."

-Hans Selye

Many people don't see the good side of things because they are too preoccupied dealing with their worries, fears, anxieties and stressors. Stress has always been perceived as something negative but it is so ironic that people always seem to look for things to stress about. When they wake up in the morning, they think of what they are going to wear, how they are going to reach their office in the fastest possible way, whom they are going to have lunch with and what time they could get back home. These simple things may seem so uncomplicated and benign, but the truth is, they can cause great worries and unnecessary stress at the end of the day.

No matter what you do, and no matter how you try to avoid it, stress will always be there, waiting around the corner for you to come and get it. In fact, you need it to function properly. For example, you are preparing for an exam or work presentation tomorrow and you are feeling some stress about it. To relieve some of the stress, what you do is you study and prepare for it. Though stress here is something that you don't see as positive, your response to it is. The next thing you know is that you did very well of the exam or presentation! Imagine if you are not worried about your exam. The most likely thing you'd do is you won't prepare for it. Sometimes, not feeling the stress is more dangerous because you don't perceive any harm and your body as a harmless situation.

Stress takes on different forms. It can be mild, which is something that you can easily overcome, or it could be something more severe, something that can exhaust you of your energy and resources. Mild stress, just like the example given above, is helpful because it keeps you prepared for what's going to happen. But if the stress is so severe that you don't know what to do anymore, then it becomes harmful.

When you feel that you can no longer perform well in your job, or when you can no longer think straight, or when you think that you are not anymore getting the results that you want to achieve, you are likely undergoing severe stress. At this point, it is not advisable to continue with what you are doing. Just like a machine that has been excessively used, people inefficiently function when they are under severe stress. Eliminating the stressors is not easy but there are ways you can do it.

Don't try to control everything

People have the tendency to control everything: their time, money, and other people. What they don't know is that they get most of the stress comes from trying to control everything. It's not bad to be carefree every once in a while. Give yourself some freedom by not thinking about your bills at home, your work deadlines and the traffic jam outside. Recognize that at the moment these things are out of your control.

You can avoid thinking about them. Change your mindset. You can use the analogy of a dresser. In the bottom drawer you can store all your stresses and worries. In the top drawer you can store all your happy thoughts and things you're grateful for. So if you're having difficulty changing your mindset or thoughts, go ahead and place them in the bottom drawer and grab something from the top one.

Spend one hour a day without technology

It is true that technology plays an important role in people's lives. However, it is also true that it takes up a large part of one's time. People are meant for interaction and socialization. Though technology, like smartphones, tablets and computers are meant for communication, people nowadays forget and do not seem to bother talking with their classmates, co-workers and neighbors. It is as if their minds have been taken over by these gadgets.

These gadgets can be a source of additional stress. Spending one hour a day (or longer) without them would be a helpful way of relieving your stress. It can be very challenging for some to not check their email or look at their phone for even one hour. Instead of interacting with your smartphone or computer, talk with the people around you, laugh out loud with them and share stories with them. You'll see how refreshing and energizing this can be.

For more information on strategies for telling stories, and strategies for talking to strangers and making new friends, check out: The Storytelling Method, and The Conversation Method, which will give your social life a new set of wings.

Take a Time Out

Time out is for those who are brave enough to take a step back and rethink of everything. Taking a timeout does not mean giving up; it just means that there are some things that you need to take care of before proceeding to the next step. In a sense, it's a way to unwind and look at the big picture and refocus on what is important about whatever you are currently working on.

Stress often results from too much work and not giving your body or mind enough time to relax. Give yourself a break from working. Taking short work breaks each hour increases productivity. Even a short 2 – 5 minute break to stretch your body, or 5 minutes to walk around or 5 minutes to step outside and get some fresh air will help. When you continue working despite exhaustion, you may produce unsatisfactory results that can further aggravate your stress. Some people like to meditate and others like to take a walk to clear their mind. So go ahead and take that time-out.

Live in the present moment

Most of the anxiety, worry, and stress that you feel arise from thinking about the future or the past. You stress about 'what if's'. What if you did this or what if you did not do that? You worry whether it's going to rain or whether you can meet the deadline of your assignment. Live in the present so that much of your worries and anxiety will be eliminated. A rule I like to use is the 80/20 rule – spending 80% of my time enjoying the present moment, and 20% of my time thinking of the future or what I can learn from my past. Life is most fun and relaxing when you are enjoying the present moment.

If you want to learn more about how to live in the present moment, I highly recommend my book titled How To Live In the Present Moment, which has proven to be an eye-opening experience for many readers.

Chapter 3: Build Your Confidence

"With everything that has happened to you, you can either feel sorry for yourself or treat what has happened as a gift. Everything is either an opportunity to grow or an obstacle to keep you from growing. You get to choose."
-Dr. Wayne W. Dyer

People have different views on how confidence is built. Some believe it comes from being popular in school or in your career. For others believe it comes from being beautiful or handsome, or being the richest in town. Or it could mean being able to accomplish something or being a member of a certain group of people. If you are going to use these definitions of confidence, it seems that it is directly associated with material and physical things. The reality is that confidence comes from within, and through this all the external things can be achieved.

Confidence is something that does not only talk about a certain aspect of a person; rather it refers to the wholeness of the person—the physical, emotional, intellectual aspects, as well as strengths and weaknesses. Appreciating who you *really* are and being able to proudly walk out into the world with *all* your attributes, both good and bad, is the real essence of self-confidence.

The advantage of improving your self-confidence is not only about being able to do *what you want*, but it also gives you a positive attitude. Imagine yourself being appointed as a leader in a team, given that you had all the qualifications. At the same time imagine that you do not believe in yourself and are not confident in your abilities, it is likely that you would refuse the position. You fear that you cannot fulfill the responsibilities associated with leadership due to your lack of self-confidence. However, you still have all the qualifications and abilities to do it, but you still resist.

You may not be the best leader at first, but you will be, and your confidence will grow as you gain more experience with the position. Confidence is built from practicing something over and over again.

On the other hand, if you are the type of person who is already confident, knowing that you have the ability and the capacity to become a leader then you would most likely accept the position and the responsibilities associated with it. With improved self-confidence, you are able to lift your spirits, believe that you can do it, and that you can accomplish whatever it is that you need to do.

Having good self-confidence can sometimes be equated with being strong and resilient. Everything that you do requires strength, not only physically, but mentally as well. The will to get up from bed early in the morning to go to work or to school is already a sign of strength. You are able to overcome the temptation of just lying in your bed, going back to sleep and spending the rest of the day being lazy. Being confident with what you do drives you to achieve your goals, work at your best and overcome any challenges that come your way. When you are confident in who *you* are, you become stronger and more resilient to adversity.

5 techniques to build confidence:

1. Be Realistic

Low self-confidence often stems from setting goals and expectations that are too high or unrealistic. Though it is helpful to aim high, it is also noteworthy to keep your goals realistic, keeping in mind *your* strengths and weaknesses. If you want to buy a house and lot worth $1,000,000 and you are just earning $5,000 a month, it is not realistic to say that you can buy that property within a few months.

When you are not able to achieve your goal within the time frame that you set, there's the tendency that you'll get discouraged and unmotivated. This will cause your self-confidence to go down. Therefore, set realistic goals – even if they seem super small because there is a sense of fulfillment from achieving goals. Again, I encourage you to set big goals, but do make them realistic, even if you have to start with tiny steps, such as setting a day and time to make a budget – in order to bring you closer to a realistic timeframe of when you can buy a house or what house you can afford.

For more information on setting goals, I highly recommend my book on Goal Setting, where it goes into detail about setting S.M.A.R.T. goals and staying motivated.

2. Acknowledge strengths and accept weaknesses

Your self-confidence is founded on your strengths and weaknesses, and it is important for you to be aware them. Know which of your characteristics need improvement and know which ones you can use to your advantage. Working your way up does not stop with just knowing them; you have to use them, improve on them and work with them. For example, you know deep down that you are a good leader. When the opportunity to lead comes your way, grab it and maximize your potential. Making use of your strengths will make you more aware of your abilities and will give you the opportunity to keep improving. Meanwhile, it is also important that you don't ignore your weaknesses. The more you challenge your weaknesses and reflect on them, the faster you will improve.

3. Don't compare

Most people love comparing themselves with other people. What makes her better? What makes him the boss' favorite? What qualities do I not have that he has? These are just some of the questions that people ask whenever they see someone they think is better than them.

Comparing yourself with other people will just highlight your weaknesses more than your strengths. It's nonsense because everyone is good at certain things and bad at other things. No one is going to be good at everything.

Instead of comparing yourself with other people, you can compare your future self to the old one. One of the great things about emotions is that they are elastic and have the ability to change if we choose to do so. You can take note of your characteristics that you want to change, work on it for the next month and then reevaluate yourself. Or you can look at yourself now and compare yourself to who you used to be. If you were once very controlling and bossy, you can ask yourself whether you still are or not. If you were once a pessimistic person, you can check-in with yourself and see if you are now an optimistic person. People change and you are not an exception. Change for the better and don't compare yourself with other people.

4. Praise and reward yourself

Negative self-talk usually arises when you feel that you are not loved or appreciated by the people around you. The reality is that you don't *need* them to make you feel better. Before looking for someone who can praise you, learn to praise yourself. Pat yourself on the shoulder or congratulate yourself for a job well done. After all, it is only you who knows how much effort and how much time you have invested. For example, when you have successfully closed a deal with your business partner, treat yourself to dinner or something special *for yourself*. Don't wait for someone else to congratulate you.

5. Be Assertive

People sometimes mistake assertiveness with aggressiveness. Assertiveness is something admirable and positive, while aggressiveness can be perceived as more negative. Being aggressive is often seen as achieving your goals however possible and in whatever way you can, even if it includes harm to others. On the other hand, assertiveness is achieving your goal with consideration for the people who are involved, making sure that no one gets hurt along the way.

A simple scenario showing the differences between being passive, aggressive, and assertive could be when you are in a hurry walking through a crowded street and someone stands in your way. There are three possible things that can happen. You can either push or shout at the person and demand that he moves; or say nothing and hope that he moves; or you can say, "Excuse me" and wait for the person to move aside. Of course, the first one might be the faster way but may cause harm, and the second would likely be ineffective, whereas the latter is the better option because you get what you want without causing harm to others. If you want to achieve something, assert yourself. This is the way to get the most effective result.

Chapter 4: Bring On Positivity

"Man often becomes what he believes himself to be. If I keep on saying to myself that I cannot do a certain thing, it is possible that I may end by really becoming incapable of doing it. On the contrary, if I have the belief that I can do it, I shall surely acquire the capacity to do it even if I may not have it at the beginning."

-Mahatma Gandhi

Optimism is not just a state of the mind; it is also shown through your actions and words. If your work gets canceled due to inclement weather, an optimistic person would enjoy the time off or work on something else to be productive. Whereas positivity is about having a positive attitude - even when challenging situations arise. One psychologist once theorized that you attract what you think about most. This is the Law of Attraction and it says that when you think of and focus on something, it will happen. Remember how you wished to not see a certain person and you did? You focused your thoughts and energy on that particular person, and there they were! Well, that's law of attraction.

This theory is true whether you are thinking negative *or* positive thoughts. The *more* you think of negative thoughts, the *more* you'll encounter negative things. Let's look at this scenario. Imagine you're in a taxi hurrying your way to work with a traffic jam on the street. Human nature tells you to start worrying because you might be late to work. When you do, you decide to get out of the cab and power-walk your way through the traffic jam. As you are walking, you keep looking at your watch, ticking and ticking. Twenty minutes until work became ten that rapidly became five. At this point you're stressed and sending out all types of negative energy. As you cross the street while looking at your watch, a car hits you. It may not be a big hit but you still felt the pain. And because you are very anxious and stressed during that time, you shout at the driver and confront him. Now the clock says you are late. With this scenario, you can see that a cascade of events will happen once you strongly think negative thoughts.

The same is true when you think of more positive thoughts. When you are about to enter your workplace, you started telling yourself that you can do all your tasks for the day. You greeted everyone with a smile on your face, found your way to your desk and pleasantly started working. Even if a pile of unfinished papers greeted you that morning, you did not panic. Instead, you took a look at each of them and prioritized them. You grouped all papers needing immediate attention and you did the same for the not-so-urgent ones. With a positive attitude, you gradually finish them all without undue stress. For more information on using words to attract more into your life, I recommend my book title The Power of NLP.

Adopting positivity, just like other processes, takes time. You need to consciously make an effort to practice it every moment of every day, whatever comes your way, until it becomes a good habit. Again, it is believed that it takes 30-days of consistently doing something to form a habit. Adopting positivity is a commitment and you have to be faithful in adopting positivity not only in your thoughts, but also in your actions and words. Below are some strategies to begin with positivity.

Be healthy

Many people don't think they can manage their problems because they are sick or because they feel too weak to accomplish their tasks. If this is the case, the best way to counteract it is to stay healthy. Start a healthy lifestyle by eating a balanced and healthy diet – one that has the right amount of carbohydrates, proteins, and other sources that is right for you. A food regimen that contains plenty of vegetables and fruits is good because they contain vitamins and minerals that are essential for the proper functioning of your cells.

Exercise is another way of maintaining a healthy lifestyle. Exercise does not only make your body stronger and your muscles larger, but exercise is a good way of relieving stress and energizing yourself. If you exercise regularly, you'll have the zest to work the whole day. Without exercise or good nutrition, you'll often feel lazy, inadequate and weak.

Change the way you think

Though changing the way you think is as difficult as changing the way you were brought up, it is something that you can achieve over time. Emotions are things that we ultimately have control over, and we have the ability to change the way we feel about certain things. Much of it can be changed shift of perspectives or the way we view certain situations. Think of ways to turn your negative thoughts into positive ones and do not let these negative thoughts control you. Ask yourself, what is one positive thing I can take out of this negative perspective? Then, look for another positive thing, and focus your energy on those positive things instead of the negative ones.

Start positive self- talk

You don't *need* other people to encourage you. You can do it to yourself. A simple "Good job!" or "Congratulations!" can already do the trick. What is even better with this method is that you don't need a specific time to do it. You can do this when you are busy, or when you are not doing anything, or when you are eating. You don't need anyone to do this, either. It may sound silly but it works. Talk to yourself like talking to a friend; encourage yourself, praise yourself and always remind yourself that you are powerful enough to overcome all the challenges that you will encounter in the future.

If you are doing something for the first time, don't be afraid. A negative self-talk may sound like, "I don't know how to do this," but a positive self-talk would say,

"This is a new experience and I will learn new things from this." If you want to do something but you don't have the resources, a negative self-talk would say, "I **cannot** do it because I need this first." A positive self-talk would most likely be, "I **can** do it. I just need to get this first."

Always look forward to something

Every day, you get to encounter different challenges, experience various events or meet new people. When you see the things happening to you as being part of something great, then you are attracting positive things into your life.

Positivity and optimism start with a positive attitude. You can gain optimism by anticipating that something good will come out of whatever it is you are going through right now.

Chapter 5

Half Empty or Half Full?

"Optimism is the most important human trait, because it allows us to evolve our ideas, to improve our situation, and to hope for a better tomorrow."

-Seth Godin

When people see a glass half-filled with water, they can see it as either half full or half empty. Seeing a glass as half empty is a sign of negativity, while seeing a glass half full is the opposite. The way you perceive this scenario reflects how you perceive your life. Take a moment and think about how you perceive the glass. Is it half full or half empty?

If you see the glass as half full, it means that you are on your way to positive thinking. It may not be as fast as pouring water into the glass until it overflows, but it is something that you can achieve with time. If you see the glass as half empty, it means that you believe there is nothing you can do to take control of your life. However, if your glass is half empty, the good news is that it is possible to change, as all emotions are flexible or elastic.

At the end of the day, when you look back on the things that have transpired or the things that you have learned, you have the choice to see the glass as half empty or half full. It is your choice, and no one else's.

Positivity is a complex that does not work without the presence of the other parts. As mentioned in the earlier parts of the book, you need to be positive not only in your thoughts, but in your words and actions as well. All these elements must work hand in hand to achieve complete optimism. Thinking positively without acting positively is useless. It is like knowing what you want but not taking action to get it. Words are as equally important because they form emotions and either help or deter you through challenging situations.

Positive self-talk is a form of catharsis that helps you express your emotions and be aware of them. Once you have acknowledged your emotions, you can easily find a way on how to address them. Then you can let go of the negative impacts of your experiences and put a more positive tone to it.

Everything is a matter of perspective. It is up to you to make the choice of how you respond to life. If you choose negative, you will lose. If you choose positive, you'll flourish.

Conclusion

A positive attitude teaches you that anything is possible. With positivity, you are confident and more willing to take on new challenges. You are ready to face the world and you will not be afraid to conquer your fears.

I encourage you to read this book again and use it as a reminder of how you can continue to implement a positive mindset. It is one of the greatest strategies that we as humans can develop and train ourselves to do.

It may not be easy to remain positive especially when tough situations arise, but remember that you have power over your emotions, and you are the only one who can control what you are doing, how you feel toward situations, and how you respond to others.

Continue to make positive thinking a daily practice until it becomes a habit, which – as stated previously – takes 30 days of conscious effort to form.

14024242R00019

Printed in Great Britain
by Amazon.co.uk, Ltd.,
Marston Gate.